JAMIE HENDRY PRODUCTIONS,
ANNERIN PRODUCTIONS,
RAIN PRODUCTIONS, BB PROMOTION,
MAGICSPACE ENTERTAINMENT,
RUBIN FOGEL &
JULIAN STONEMAN ASSOCIATES
PRESENT

ORIGINAL UK COMPANY
EMANUELE ANGELETTI   JOHN BROSNAN
GORDON ELSMORE   JAMES FOX
MICHAEL GAGLIANO   IAN B. GARCIA
REUVEN GERSHON   STEPHEN HILL   PHIL MARTIN
RYAN ALEX FARMERY   MICHAEL BRAMWELL

SCENIC DESIGNER
TIM McQUILLEN-WRIGHT
GLOBAL LIGHTING DESIGNER
STEPHAN GOTSCHEL
UK LIGHTING DESIGNER
HUMPHREY McDERMOTT
SOUND DESIGNER
GARETH OWEN
UK MUSICAL SUPERVISOR & RESIDENT DIRECTOR
JOHN MAHER
VIDEO DESIGNERS
DARREN McCAULLEY
MATHIEU ST-ARNAUD

LET IT BE

CASTING DIRECTOR
PIPPA AILION
COSTUME SUPERVISOR
JACK GALLOWAY
PRODUCTION/CREATIVE DIRECTOR
SCOTT CHRISTENSEN
PRODUCTION MANAGER
PATRICK MOLONY
PRESS & PR
THE CORNER SHOP PR
MARKETING CONSULTANT
MARTIN BARROW
MARKETING & ADVERTISING
AKA
GENERAL MANAGER
JAMIE HENDRY PRODUCTIONS
DIRECTOR & MUSICAL SUPERVISOR
JOEY CURATOLO
CREATED AND CONCEIVED BY

RAIN

MARK LEWIS   JOEY CURATOLO   RALPH CASTELLI
JOE BITHORN   STEVE LANDES

WISE PUBLICATIONS
part of The Music Sales Group
London/New York/Paris/Sydney/Copenhagen/
Berlin/Madrid/Hong Kong/Tokyo

Published by
Wise Publications
14-15 Berners Street, London W1T 3LJ, UK.

Exclusive Distributors:
Music Sales Limited
Distribution Centre, Newmarket Road,
Bury St Edmunds, Suffolk IP33 3YB, UK.
Music Sales Pty Limited
20 Resolution Drive, Caringbah, NSW 2229, Australia.

Order No. NO91652
ISBN: 978-1-78038-781-9
This book © Copyright 2012 Wise Publications,
a division of Music Sales Limited.

Edited by Jenni Norey.
Photographers: Brinkhoff/Mögenburg.
Printed in the EU.

SHE LOVES YOU

WORDS & MUSIC BY JOHN LENNON & PAUL McCARTNEY

PLEASE PLEASE ME

WORDS & MUSIC BY JOHN LENNON & PAUL McCARTNEY

Come on. (Come on.)___ Come on. (Come on.)___ Come

on. (Come on.)___ Come on. (Come on.)___ Please, please me, oh

yeah, like I please you.

I don't want to sound com-plain-ing but you know there's al-ways rain in

D.S. al Coda   Coda

FROM ME TO YOU

WORDS & MUSIC BY JOHN LENNON & PAUL McCARTNEY

I WANT TO HOLD YOUR HAND

WORDS & MUSIC BY JOHN LENNON & PAUL McCARTNEY

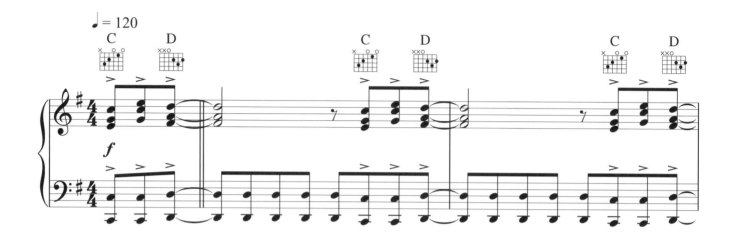

21

THIS BOY

WORDS & MUSIC BY JOHN LENNON & PAUL McCARTNEY

A HARD DAY'S NIGHT

WORDS & MUSIC BY JOHN LENNON & PAUL McCARTNEY

So why on earth should I moan,___ 'cause when I get you a - lone___ you know I feel___ O.___ K.___ When I'm home___

I'M HAPPY JUST TO DANCE WITH YOU

WORDS & MUSIC BY JOHN LENNON & PAUL McCARTNEY

Be - fore this dance is through,___ I think I'll love you too;___ I'm so

YESTERDAY

WORDS & MUSIC BY JOHN LENNON & PAUL McCARTNEY

HELP!

WORDS & MUSIC BY JOHN LENNON & PAUL McCARTNEY

1, 3. When I_____ was young - er, so_____ much young - er than_____ to - day,_____
2. And now____ my life has changed in, oh, so man - y ways,___

I nev - er need - ed an - y - bod - y's
my in - de - pen - dence seems____ to

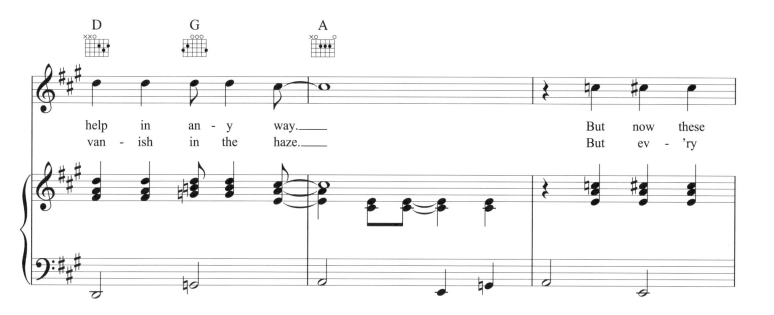

help in an - y way.____ But now these
van - ish in the haze.____ But ev - 'ry

DAY TRIPPER

WORDS & MUSIC BY JOHN LENNON & PAUL McCARTNEY

Moderate Rock

1. Got a good rea - son   for
2. She's a big teas - er,
3. Tried to please her,

It took me so_____ long___ to find out___

and I found out.

out.

TWIST AND SHOUT

WORDS & MUSIC BY BERT RUSSELL & PHIL MEDLEY

Just like I knew you would. (Like I knew you would.

And let me know that you're mine. (Let me know you're mine.

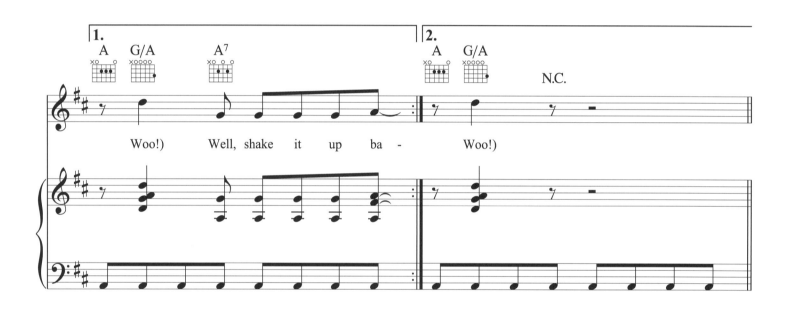

1.
A G/A   A⁷

Woo!) Well, shake it up ba -

2.
A G/A   N.C.

Woo!)

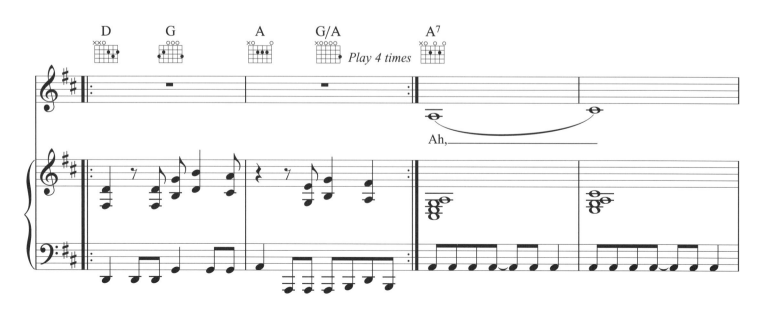

D   G   A   G/A   *Play 4 times*   A⁷

Ah,

SGT. PEPPER'S LONELY HEARTS CLUB BAND

WORDS & MUSIC BY JOHN LENNON & PAUL McCARTNEY

Moderately slow, with a strong beat

1. It was twen-ty years a-go to-day___ that Ser-geant Pep-per taught the band to play.___ They've been

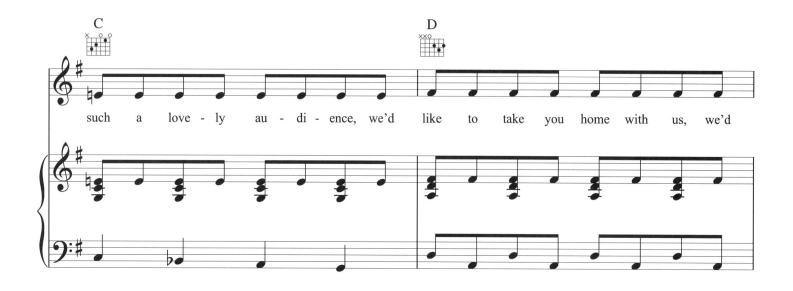

such a love - ly au - di - ence, we'd like to take you home with us, we'd

love to take you home. 2. I don't real - ly want to stop the show_ but I

thought you might like to know_ that the sing - er's going to sing a song_ and he

wants you all to sing a - long.____ So let me in-tro-duce to you____ the

one and on - ly Bil - ly Shears;____ and Ser - geant Pep-per's Lone - ly Hearts Club

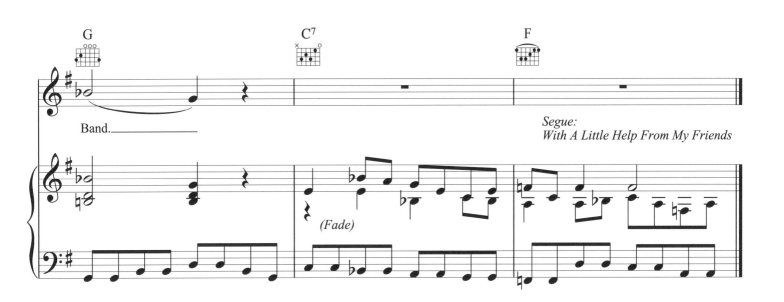

Band._____

Segue:
With A Little Help From My Friends

(Fade)

WITH A LITTLE HELP FROM MY FRIENDS

WORDS & MUSIC BY JOHN LENNON & PAUL McCARTNEY

LUCY IN THE SKY WITH DIAMONDS

WORDS & MUSIC BY JOHN LENNON & PAUL McCARTNEY

ELEANOR RIGBY

WORDS & MUSIC BY JOHN LENNON & PAUL McCARTNEY

WHEN I'M SIXTY FOUR

WORDS & MUSIC BY JOHN LENNON & PAUL McCARTNEY

When I get old - er, los - ing my hair_ man - y years from now;___

sim.

We shall scrimp and save;___
Grand-child-ren on your knee;___ Ve - ra,
Chuck and Dave.

four?

SGT. PEPPER'S LONELY HEARTS CLUB BAND (REPRISE)

WORDS & MUSIC BY JOHN LENNON & PAUL McCARTNEY

A DAY IN THE LIFE

WORDS & MUSIC BY JOHN LENNON & PAUL MCCARTNEY

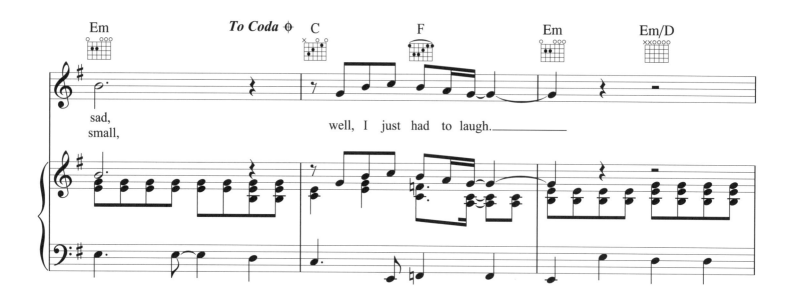

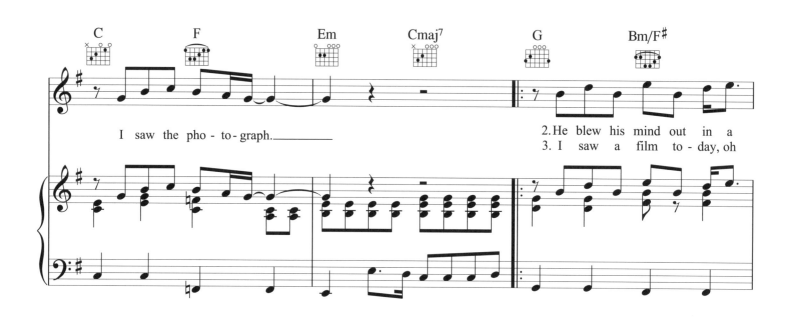

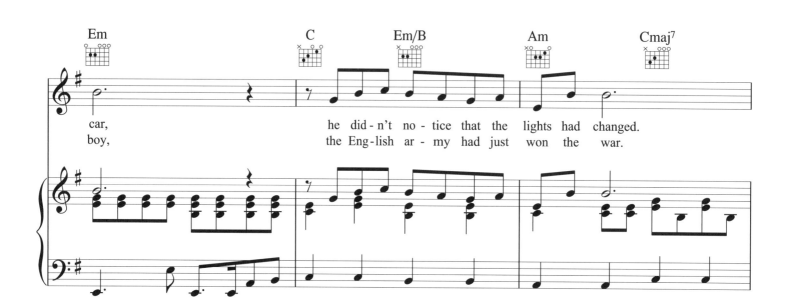

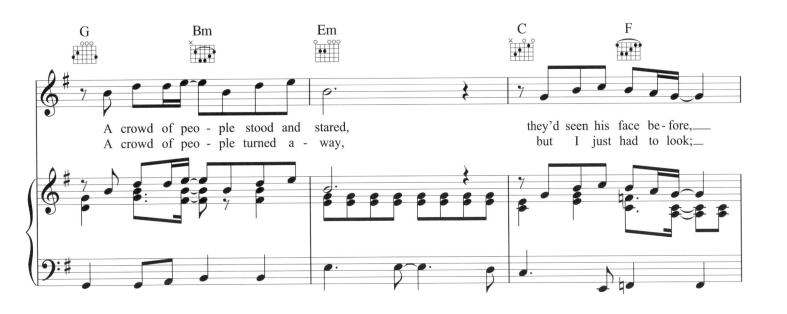

A crowd of peo - ple stood and stared,
A crowd of peo - ple turned a - way,

they'd seen his face be - fore,
but I just had to look;

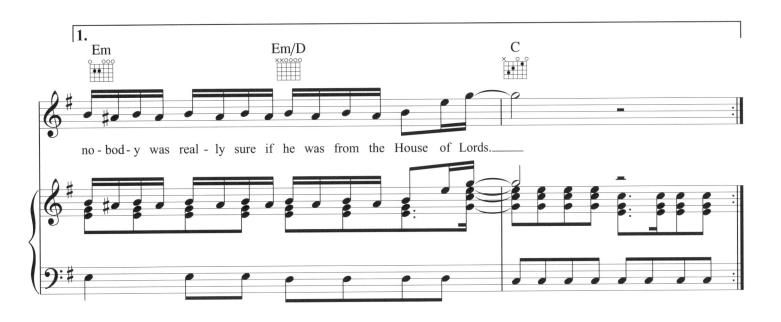

1.

no - bod - y was real - ly sure if he was from the House of Lords.

2.

hav - ing read the book. I'd love to turn

they had to count them all.___ Now they know how man-y holes it takes to fill the Al - bert

Hall. I'd love to turn___ you___ on.___

ALL YOU NEED IS LOVE

WORDS & MUSIC BY JOHN LENNON & PAUL McCARTNEY

1. There's noth-ing you can do   that can't be   done._____
2. There's noth-ing you can make   that can't be   made._____
3. There's noth-ing you can know   that is - n't   known._____

MAGICAL MYSTERY TOUR

WORDS & MUSIC BY JOHN LENNON & PAUL McCARTNEY

coming to take you away.
dying to take you away.

Coming to take you a-
Dying to take you a-

1. -way.

2. -way, take you to-day.

N.C.

Repeat ad lib. to fade

92

STRAWBERRY FIELDS FOREVER

WORDS & MUSIC BY JOHN LENNON & PAUL McCARTNEY

Straw - ber - ry Fields___ for - ev - er,___

Straw - ber - ry Fields___ for -

- ev - er,___

Straw - ber - ry Fields___ for - ev - er.___

To fade ad lib.

96

BLACKBIRD

WORDS & MUSIC BY JOHN LENNON & PAUL McCARTNEY

1. Black-bird sing-ing in the dead of night
2. Black-bird sing-ing in the dead of night

(3° instrumental)

Take these bro-ken wings___ and learn to fly;___
Take these sunk-en eyes___ and learn to see;___

all your life_____ you were on-ly wait-ing for this mo-ment to a-
all your life_____ you were on-ly wait-ing for this mo-ment to be

TWO OF US

WORDS & MUSIC BY JOHN LENNON & PAUL McCARTNEY

IN MY LIFE

WORDS & MUSIC BY JOHN LENNON & PAUL McCARTNEY

HERE COMES THE SUN

WORDS & MUSIC BY GEORGE HARRISON

Here comes_ the sun,____ doo da doo doo. Here comes_ the sun,____ and I say

"It's all____ right."

and I say "It's all right."

Sun, sun, sun, here it comes.

110

WHILE MY GUITAR GENTLY WEEPS

WORDS & MUSIC BY GEORGE HARRISON

(1.) look at___ you___ all,_____ see the love___ there___ that's sleep - ing,
(2.) look at___ the___ world,_____ and I no - tice___ it's turn - ing,
(3.) look at___ you___ all,_____ see the love___ there___ that's sleep - ing,

COME TOGETHER

WORDS & MUSIC BY JOHN LENNON & PAUL McCARTNEY

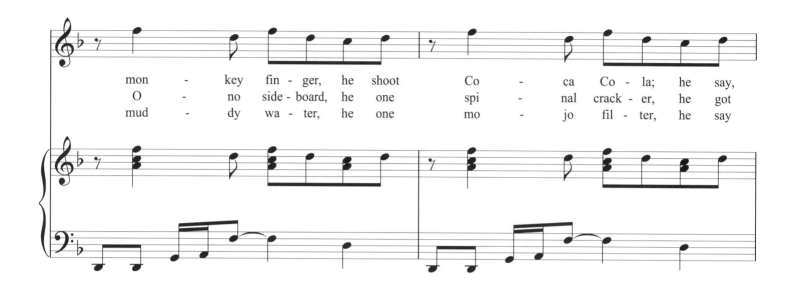

mon - key fin - ger, he shoot Co - ca Co - la; he say,
O - no side - board, he one spi - nal crack - er, he got
mud - dy wa - ter, he one mo - jo fil - ter, he say

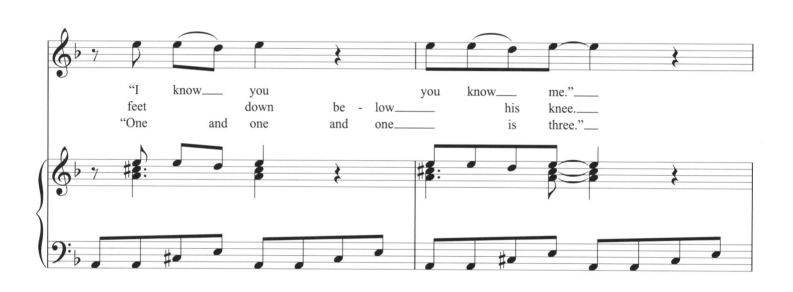

"I know___ you you know___ me."___
feet down be - low___ his knee.___
"One and one and one___ is three."___

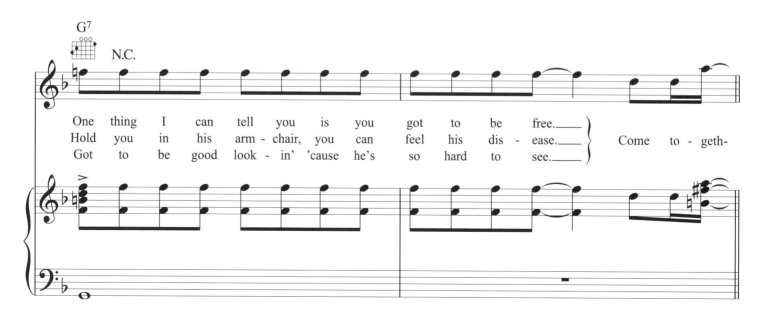

G7
N.C.

One thing I can tell you is you got to be free.___
Hold you in his arm - chair, you can feel his dis - ease.___ Come to - geth -
Got to be good look - in' 'cause he's so hard to see.___

GET BACK

WORDS & MUSIC BY JOHN LENNON & PAUL McCARTNEY

Jo Jo was a man who thought___ he was a lon-er, but___ he knew it could-n't last.___

to where you once be - longed.____ Get back,____ get back,____

back____ to where you once be - longed.____

Get back Joe.____

REVOLUTION

WORDS & MUSIC BY JOHN LENNON & PAUL McCARTNEY

THE END

WORDS & MUSIC BY JOHN LENNON & PAUL McCARTNEY

Love you,_____ love you,_____

GIVE PEACE A CHANCE

WORDS & MUSIC BY JOHN LENNON

rag - is - m, tag - is - m, this - is - m, that - is - m, is-n't it the most?

All we___ are say - - - -ing___ is give peace___ a

chance.___

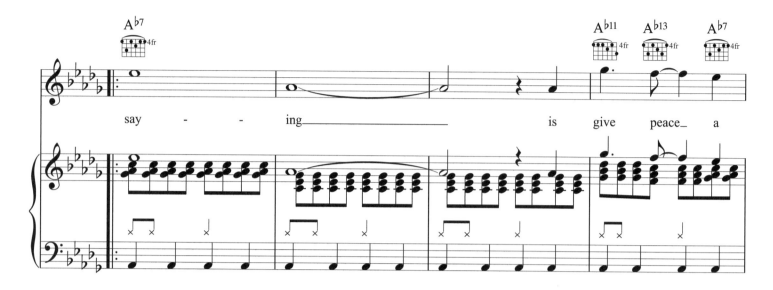

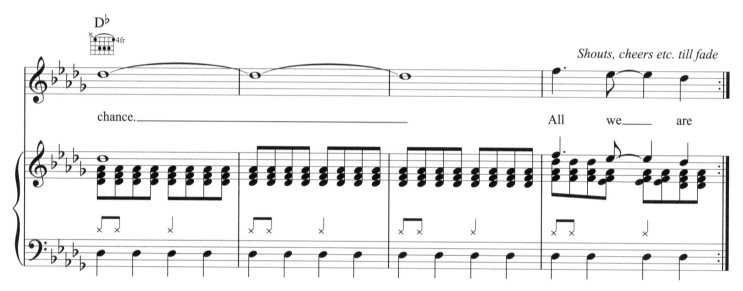

Verse 2:
Everybody's talking about ministers, sinisters, banisters and canisters
Bishops and fishops, rabbis and popeyes, bye bye bye.

Verse 3:
Everybody's talking about revolution, evolution, mastication, flagellation
Regulation, intergration, meditations, United Nations, congratulations.

Verse 4:
Everybody's talking about John and Yoko, Timmy Leary, Rosemary, Tommy Smothers
Bobby Dylan, Tommy Cooper, Derek Taylor, Norman Mailer,
Alan Ginsberg, Hare Krishna, Hare, Hare Krishna.

LET IT BE

WORDS & MUSIC BY JOHN LENNON & PAUL McCARTNEY

find my-self__ in times__ of trou-ble, Moth-er Mar-y comes__ to me, speak-ing words of wis-dom. Let it
(2.) when the bro - ken heart - ed peo - ple liv-ing in__ the world__ a - gree, there will be an an - swer. Let it
(3.) when the night__ is cloud - y there is still a light__ that shines__ on me, shine un - til to - mor-row. Let it

HEY JUDE

WORDS & MUSIC BY JOHN LENNON & PAUL McCARTNEY

123456789

SHE LOVES YOU
PLEASE PLEASE ME
FROM ME TO YOU
I WANT TO HOLD YOUR HAND
THIS BOY
A HARD DAY'S NIGHT
I'M HAPPY JUST TO DANCE WITH YOU
YESTERDAY
HELP! • DAY TRIPPER
TWIST AND SHOUT
SGT. PEPPER'S LONELY HEARTS CLUB BAND
WITH A LITTLE HELP
FROM MY FRIENDS
LUCY IN THE SKY WITH DIAMONDS
ELEANOR RIGBY
WHEN I'M SIXTY FOUR
SGT. PEPPER'S LONELY HEARTS CLUB BAND (REPRISE)
A DAY IN THE LIFE
ALL YOU NEED IS LOVE
MAGICAL MYSTERY TOUR
STRAWBERRY FIELDS FOREVER
BLACKBIRD
TWO OF US • IN MY LIFE
HERE COMES THE SUN
WHILE MY GUITAR GENTLY WEEPS
COME TOGETHER • GET BACK
REVOLUTION • THE END
GIVE PEACE A CHANCE
LET IT BE • HEY JUDE

ALL THE SONGS
FROM THE HIT SHOW
ARRANGED FOR
PIANO, VOICE AND GUITAR

1962-2012
50th
ANNIVERSARY
CELEBRATIONS

WISE PUBLICATIONS
part of The Music Sales Group
NO91652
www.musicsales.com

ISBN 978-1-78038-781-9

9 781780 387819